Dangerous Creatures

of the
Grasslands

Helen Bateman and Jayne Denshire

Smart Apple Media

Smart Apple Media
1980 Lookout Drive
North Mankato
Minnesota 56003

First published in 2005 by
MACMILLAN EDUCATION AUSTRALIA PTY LTD
627 Chapel Street, South Yarra 3141

Visit our website at www.macmillan.com.au

Associated companies and representatives throughout the world.

J 591.74
BAT
C.4

Library of Congress Cataloging-in-Publication Data

Bateman, Helen.
  Of the grasslands / by Helen Bateman and Jayne Denshire.
  p. cm. – (Dangerous creatures)
  Includes index.

  ISBN 1-58340-765-0

  1. Grassland animals—Juvenile literature. 2. Dangerous animals—Juvenile literature.
  I. Denshire, Jayne. II. Title.
  QL115.3B38 2005
  691.74—dc22

                                        2005042860

Project management by Limelight Press Pty Ltd
Design by Stan Lamond, Lamond Art & Design
Illustrations by Edwina Riddell
Maps by Laurie Whiddon, Map Illustrations. Adapted by Lamond Art & Design
Research by Kate McAllan

Consultant: George McKay PhD, Conservation Biologist

Printed in China

Acknowledgments
The authors and the publisher are grateful to the following for permission to reproduce copyright material:

Cover photograph: lion stalking through grass, courtesy of Paul A. Souders APL/Corbis.

Greg Fyfe/ANTPhoto.com p. 28; Ferrero-Labat/AUSCAPE pp. 9; 19; Mike Gillam/AUSCAPE p. 29; APL/Corbis/Yann Arthus-Bertrand p. 10-11; APL/Corbis/Tom Brakefield p. 22-23; APL/Corbis/D. Robert Franz p. 24; APL/Corbis/Martin Harvey p. 16; APL/Corbis/Joe McDonald pp. 18, 20-21; APL/Corbis/Carl Purcell p. 5; APL/Corbis/Winifred Wisniewski p. 7; APL/Corbis/Lynda Richardson p. 13; APL/Corbis/Patrick Robert p. 26-27; APL/Corbis/Albrecht G. Schaefer p. 17; APL/Corbis/Jeff Vanuga p. 25; PhotoDisc pp. 6, 8, 9, 15; Digital Stock pp. 10 (left), 10 (centre), 12; Corbis p. 12 (right), 14; Mark Jones/Roving Tortoise p. 23.

While every care has been taken to trace and acknowledge copyright, the publisher tenders their apologies for any accidental infringement where copyright has proved untraceable. Where the attempt has been unsuccessful, the publisher welcomes information that would redress the situation.

Please note
At the time of printing, the Internet addresses appearing in this book were correct. Owing to the dynamic nature of the Internet, however, we cannot guarantee that all these addresses will remain correct.

Contents

When a word is printed in **bold**, you can look up its meaning in the Glossary on page 31.

01191591979

Life in the grasslands

Grasslands are open, flat areas where grasses grow and trees are limited. They are found in many parts of the world and are home to many different animals. Savannah grasslands grow in hot places where a medium amount of rain falls. Grasses survive in these areas because they do not need as much moisture to grow as large trees do. For plant-eaters in these regions grass provides food, and for smaller creatures, it also offers protection as a place to live.

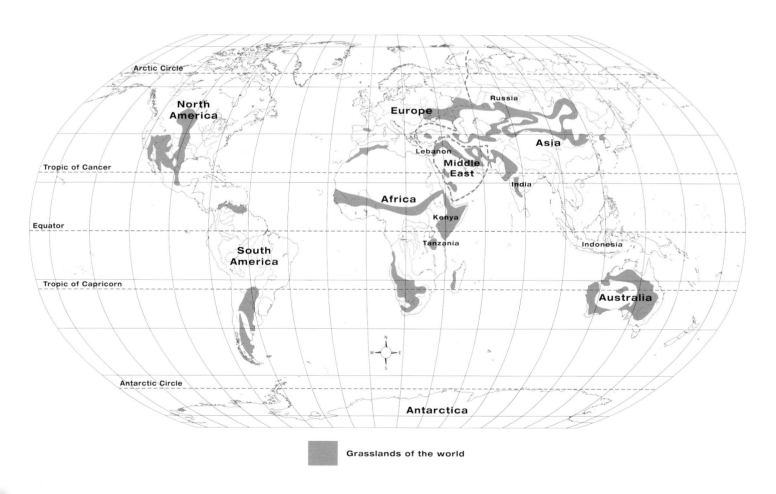

Grasslands of the world

▲ There are two main types of grassland: temperate and tropical. Temperate grasslands grow where there are wet springs followed by warm, dry summers. Tropical grasslands grow where the climate is hot, with a wet and dry season.

▲ Large herds of animals, such as white-bearded wildebeests, graze on grass in the hot savannah grasslands of Africa.

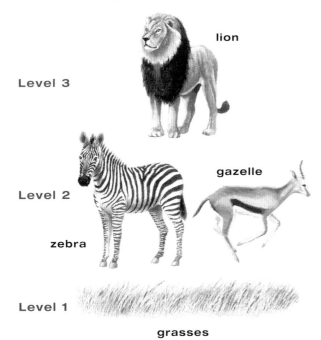

lion

Level 3

gazelle

Level 2

zebra

Level 1

grasses

▲ In this grassland food chain, animals get their food from the level below them to survive.

Danger or survival?

Animals living in the grasslands behave dangerously because they need to survive in their **habitat**. All creatures have to find food and shelter and often need to defend themselves against other animals at the same time. For many creatures, it is a case of kill or be killed.

The grasslands are home to plant-eating and meat-eating animals. The plant-eaters, called **herbivores**, depend on grass as their food. They attract large numbers of meat-eaters, called **carnivores**, who eat them. The herbivores must always be on the lookout for carnivores in search of a meal. Yet the carnivores face danger from the herbivores because the plant-eaters do not give up without a fight.

In this survival cycle, which is called a **food chain**, plants are eaten by herbivores who are in turn eaten by carnivores. Animals higher up the food chain survive by eating animals in the level below them.

African lions

VITAL STATISTICS

LENGTH
up to eight feet
(2.5 m)

WEIGHT
up to 551 pounds
(250 kg)

WHERE FOUND
central, eastern,
and southern Africa

Lions are the largest and one of the most dangerous **predators** in the grasslands. Their powerful size, strong jaws, and razor-sharp teeth earn them the reputation as king of all beasts. They spend their days lying hidden behind rocks or wandering across the plains in search of prey. Female lions, or lionesses, live in a **pride** of up to six, along with their cubs. The males visit their pride to mate, or to feed.

Lions often like to hunt after nightfall because, like most cats, they see well in the dark.

▲ Male lions often feed off the prey that the lionesses have caught. Plant-eating animals, such as zebras, often fall victim to the lion's jaws.

Grassland warrior

A lion's body is built for its life as a hunter. Its hind limbs are strong and sturdy with powerful muscles that help it sprint as it comes in for the kill. It uses its front limbs to seize its **prey** before cutting through its victim's body with its scissor-like teeth. A male lion is most easily identified by its thick mane. The lion's sandy-coloured fur is ideal **camouflage**, keeping it hidden as it **stalks** its prey. Its whiskers are very sensitive and help the lion to sense where on the victim to grip its jaws.

▲ Lions can be a danger to each other. Females will fight with males from another pride to protect their young or keep food safe.

Strong females

Lionesses are the main hunters and they usually hunt as a pack. Once they spot their victim, they spread out around it so that it can be caught if it tries to get away. Lions pull their victim to the ground, then grab the animal by the throat in their jaws, often suffocating it before it bleeds to death.

DANGER REPORT

In 1898, a series of vicious lion attacks occurred in Kenya. Indian workers were building a railway track about 25 miles (40 km) north of the Tsavo National Park. It is thought that two lions from the park killed more than 26 Indians and a number of Africans from this railway building project. The lions were finally shot.

fact flash

Lion cubs practice the hunting skills they will need when they grow up by stalking, chasing, and pouncing on each other.

Cheetahs

VITAL STATISTICS

LENGTH
up to five feet (1.5 m)

WEIGHT
up to 159 pounds
(72 kg)

WHERE FOUND
eastern and
southern Africa

Wide, open grasslands are ideal for the life of cheetahs. They survive by running down their prey at high speed before coming in for the attack. Their long legs allow them to run fast, making them the fastest land animals in the world. Their sharp claws help them to grip the ground as they sprint in pursuit of their prey. These swift, big cats live together in **lairs**, usually near patches of denser vegetation, which provide protection.

Speed machines

Cheetahs have a very flexible spine. This allows them to push off the ground, then pull down again as they move rapidly toward their victim. Their eyes sit at the front of their skull, giving them excellent vision for spotting prey and judging distances. Their long, strong tails steer them in the right direction, and the white tip is easy for their cubs to spot. They can run at 68 miles (110 km) per hour for about 20 seconds, then quickly lose their energy.

◀ Hidden low in the grass, the cheetah stalks its victim until it is 328 feet (100 m) away, then breaks into a chase before attacking it.

► A cheetah cub practices its hunting skills on an injured gazelle fawn. The mother cheetah sometimes catches the gazelle first, then lets it go near her cub.

◄ A mother cheetah must leave her cubs to hunt for food. Sometimes other predators will find and kill the cubs while she is away.

On the hunt

Cheetahs hunt mostly during the day. They often go after faster animals, such as Thompson's gazelles and antelopes, that can escape the grip of slower predators. After they stalk the animal, cheetahs knock it to the ground then suffocate it by grabbing its neck in their strong jaws.

◄ When the cheetah runs, its body moves like a spring, crouching close and low with one movement then stretching out long and high for the next.

Spotted hyenas

Female hyenas are happy to feed each other's cubs with milk so that each mother can hunt while her cubs are being looked after in the clan den.

VITAL STATISTICS

LENGTH
up to four feet (1.3 m)

WEIGHT
up to 154 pounds
(70 kg)

WHERE FOUND
central, eastern
and southern Africa

Spotted hyenas are both killers and **scavengers**. They are the most common meat-eaters living in the African grasslands. When they are scavenging by day, they make a loud, whooping sound to tell others in their pack that there is food nearby. Hyenas use their powerful sense of smell to sniff out blood from a distance. Then they often approach the kill of another predator, such as a lion, and drive the predator away. Hyenas live together in a **clan**.

▶ The large, round shape of hyenas' ears help them to hear each other's calls from several miles away.

◀ When a spotted hyena yawns, it exposes its sharp, bone-crushing teeth. With these teeth, it is able to eat parts of its prey that other predators cannot.

Bone crushers

Spotted hyenas are able to digest the bones and teeth of their prey, unlike other animals. This makes their droppings white. Their strong feet help them run fast and they use their well-adapted **sensory organs** to find food. Their stomach works very efficiently so they can digest their prey.

Fast food

In just over half an hour, a pack of 25 spotted hyenas can leave nothing but bones from four zebra bodies. When these predators hunt, they try to separate their victim from the herd. Then they chase it until it is exhausted and unable to get away. They drag it to the ground and kill it with one bite, then devour the remains.

fact flash

A hyena is able to eat up to one-third of its body weight in one meal.

◄ Despite the wildebeest's size, it will often fall victim to the sharp teeth of the spotted hyena. Once the hyena has the wildebeest in its clutches, there is no escape.

Plains zebras

VITAL STATISTICS

LENGTH
up to eight feet
(2.5 m)

WEIGHT
up to 849 pounds
(385 kg)

WHERE FOUND
eastern and
southern Africa

Zebras need to protect themselves from attack by their enemies. They are dangerous to their predators because of how they do this. Plains zebras live on the vast African plains and feed on grasses in the open woodlands during the hot dry weather. They then **migrate** to where the lush green grass grows on the plains once the wet weather comes. There are lots of smaller animals around during this time so larger plant-eating animals, such as zebras, are often safe from predators.

▶ Zebras run up to 25 miles (40 km) an hour when they travel long distances trying to escape danger. Foals stand within minutes of birth and learn to run within half an hour.

◀ Zebras live in large herds with a male and up to 12 females and their foals. The male keeps a close watch for predators.

Confusing the enemy

A zebra's greatest weapon is its stripes. The markings of the plains zebra are different to those of the mountain zebra and Grevy's zebra. Broad bands cover the plains zebra's main body with narrower markings on its legs and face. When a herd stands together it is well camouflaged, which makes it hard for predators to see where one zebra starts and another ends.

Deadly protection

In the dry season, zebras often dig out pits in the ground in search of water. They fight off other animals to keep them away from this water. Zebras will also give a powerful kick to a predator, such as a lion, if the lion tries to attack. These kicks have been known to break a lion's jaw, which can mean death for the lion as it can no longer hunt.

▲ Male zebras fight each other over the mares in the herd. They stand upright, then kick and bite each other, often leaving bad wounds.

fact flash

A zebra's eyes are at the side of its head, giving it a wider view. Its pupils are rectangular.

African elephants

VITAL STATISTICS

LENGTH
up to 16 feet (5 m)

WEIGHT
up to seven tons (7 t)

WHERE FOUND
central and
southern Africa

Elephants are the largest land animals and even though they are plant-eaters, they have little to fear from meat-eating predators because of their massive size. Their tusks, and their powerful trunks often ten feet (3 m) long, discourage other creatures from hunting them down, no matter how fierce these hunters may be. Like many animal communities, male elephants do not live in the herd with the females. They visit only when it is time to mate.

▲ Male elephants, called bulls, will charge each other with their tusks, to claim their female in the herd. The fighting bulls can injure each other so badly that they die.

Big and strong

An elephant's massive body weight is supported by very sturdy legs. It can run up to 19 miles (30 km) per hour, especially when it is charging its enemy. Elephants flap their ears to cool down and will hold them back to scare off their enemies. Their tusks, which are really oversized teeth, help ward off their attackers. They will also use them to spear their enemy when fighting. Their trunks are so powerful that they can kill other creatures with a single blow. During the mating season, they make more than 30 different sounds with their trunks including roars, screams, bellows, and rumbles.

Scare tactics

Elephants often try to scare their enemies by kicking up huge clouds of dust and throwing it in the air with their trunks. They will also uproot small trees and bushes with one pull, and hurl them around. When a member of the herd dies, sometimes the others bury it by breaking off tree branches with their tusks and placing them gently over the body.

Komodo dragons

VITAL STATISTICS

LENGTH
up to ten feet (3 m)

WEIGHT
up to 154 pounds
(70 kg)

WHERE FOUND
Indonesia

Komodo dragons are the world's largest lizards. They live on the Flores islands of Indonesia, where they are the main predators. These vicious creatures are strong enough to attack a water buffalo and devour it in one meal. They are also dangerous to humans, so people who live on these islands build their homes on stilts above the ground to escape them. When komodo dragons hatch they are about 16 inches (40 cm) long. Their parents are a danger to them because they eat them, so the young dragons must move away and roll themselves in dung. The dung protects the young as the komodo dragon parents do not like its smell.

Not a pretty sight

Komodo dragons are very ugly. They have dry, leathery skin and flabby necks with sharp teeth and large eyes. Their teeth carry lots of germs, left from old bits of rotten meat that get caught in their mouth. If a victim is wounded, it will die after a week or so because the germs from the komodo's teeth cause an infection.

▲ The komodo dragon's tongue acts a bit like a nose, helping it to smell rotten meat up to three miles (5 km) away. Its tongue divides at the end, like a fork.

DANGER REPORT

In 2003, it was reported that a komodo dragon had found its way into the city of Beirut in Lebanon and was terrorizing the locals. It was believed to have been brought from Indonesia into Lebanon by a German. The giant lizard had reportedly eaten a number of cats, a dog, and a horse, and had even swam in someone's swimming pool. The creature was eventually caught.

fact flash

Komodo dragons cannot chew so they use their jagged teeth to first cut the meat off their prey. Then they throw the pieces into the air, catch them and swallow them whole.

Vicious attackers

Komodo dragons will attack goats and buffalo, often knocking them down, then tearing them apart. During mating season, male dragons fight each other for the females by balancing up on their tails, then scratching and biting with their claws and teeth. Their opponent can get badly wounded, but they rarely die from the injuries.

▲ Komodo dragons compete for their kill with other dragons. They open their jaws extra wide, which lets a lot of food go down quickly.

Birds of prey

This group of birds are meat-eaters and hunt a variety of animals for their food. The largest group of birds of prey is the **raptors**, which include eagles, hawks, and vultures.

Martial eagles

Martial eagles soar high over the grassy plains in search of prey. They hunt in the savannah grasslands but often make nests in the woodlands. They hunt alone but patrol an area with a partner.

Killers of the sky

Martial eagles are very strong. They are able to knock down and kill animals as large as antelope and goats. They have excellent eyesight and can see their victim from as far away as three miles (5 km). They spot their prey from high in the air and swoop in for the kill with their wings folded back. Then they grab their prey in their strong talons, or claws. Their beaks pull the flesh apart, ready for eating.

▲ This gazelle has fallen victim to the clutches of the martial eagle. Gazelles must always be on the lookout for eagle attacks from the sky.

fact flash
Martial eagles use their strong talons to carry animals that can weigh up to seven pounds (3 kg).

Secretary birds

Secretary birds are one of the few raptors who spot their prey from the ground.

VITAL STATISTICS

LENGTH
up to five feet (1.5 m)

WINGSPAN
up to seven feet (2.15 m)

WHERE FOUND
North and southern Africa

Ground attackers

Secretary birds use their long, powerful legs to chase their victim. They swallow smaller creatures, such as insects and **rodents**, alive and whole. If an animal is bigger, such as a snake, they will stamp on it until it is dead then hold the dead creature with their toes and pull off bits of meat with their hooked beak. When these birds are mating, they perform a type of dance in the air by circling each other and crying out with a croaking call. They spend the rest of the time on the ground, even when they are fighting. Sometimes people mistake these birds for cranes or storks because of their long legs, stubby toes and long, thin tail.

DANGER REPORT

In 2003, an observer in Kruger National Park in Australia witnessed a secretary bird fiercely attack a martial eagle. The observer saw the secretary bird flip backward with its wings held open and high, then draw its legs up, ready to kick the martial eagle. It is thought that the secretary bird probably wanted the eagle's prey.

▲ This bird's name comes from its crest of feathers, which looks like the feathered pens secretaries used to tuck behind their ears.

VITAL STATISTICS
LENGTH
up to 2.5 feet (81 cm)
WINGSPAN
up to seven feet
(2.14 m)
WHERE FOUND
Russian steppes,
Africa and India

▼ The steppe eagle also hunts on the ground. It stands outside a burrow waiting for its prey to come out. When the animal appears, the eagle pounces.

Steppe eagles

Steppe eagles are always on the lookout for prey. They are ready to dive at their victim once they have spotted it from high in the air. They move from place to place, depending on the time of year and amount of food available. In Summer they breed in the steppe grasslands between Russia and Mongolia. They then migrate south to the savannah of eastern and central Africa, and parts of India, in search of prey once the harsh Winter hits.

A view from above

These birds of prey have excellent eyesight and can see their prey from 656 feet (200 m) above the ground. Many creatures live in the grasslands during Summer so there is always plenty of food, such as bushy-tailed rodents, for the steppe eagles. Once Winter comes the smaller animals die off or **hibernate**, so the eagles fly to Africa to find insects and locusts instead.

Burrowing owls

Burrowing owls live in burrows that have been abandoned by other animals, such as foxes and skunks. The owls often dig out the burrows with their talons to make them bigger, then use feathers and dung to line them, ready for their eggs.

VITAL STATISTICS
LENGTH
up to 11 inches (28 cm)
WINGSPAN
up to 24 inches (61 cm)
WHERE FOUND
North and South America

Hunters up high

These owls are both hunters from the air and on the ground, and they will attack small **mammals** as well as insects. During the breeding season, the male owls often defend the females that sit on their eggs in their nests from predators. Snakes, ferrets, and skunks will easily attack the eggs and the chicks, once they hatch. If the male sees a predator coming close to the burrow, it will scratch at it with its sharp talons. This sends the predator away.

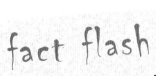
Burrowing owl chicks make a sound like a rattlesnake, which probably frightens many dangerous predators away.

▲ Burrowing owls hold their prey in their beak, then pull it apart with their talons. Sometimes smaller creatures are swallowed whole.

► Owls can see well straight ahead because their eyes are in front, but they must turn their head to the side to look around.

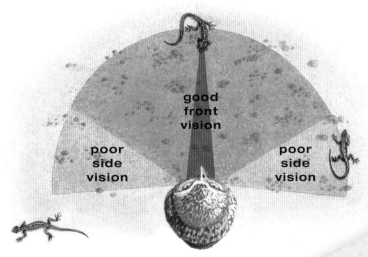

good front vision

poor side vision

poor side vision

Maned wolves

VITAL STATISTICS

LENGTH
up to four feet (1.3 m)

WEIGHT
up to 51 pounds
(23 kg)

WHERE FOUND
central and eastern
South America

Maned wolves hunt small mammals, yet are shy creatures who live within their own territory. Their name comes from the crop of thick black hair that runs down their back and looks a bit like a mane. They are **nocturnal** hunters, resting during the day under thick foliage and hunting at night. A single maned wolf will stay on the edge of a territory, waiting to fill a space in the pack which is created when a member dies or is abandoned. They are **omnivores**, eating both fruit and meat, depending on supply.

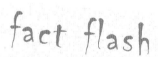

► Male and female maned wolves usually defend a territory in pairs, although they wander alone, day to day. They come together to mate, but will part again soon after.

fact flash

Some people believe that if a snakebite victim eats two pieces of a maned wolf's heart, they will not die.

Sharp sensors

Maned wolves rely on their senses to find their prey. They use their long, pointed nose to sniff out prey and their bright, orange-red eyes will spot any movement in the grass.

Their long legs are covered in short, black hair. They allow the wolf to stand high and see over long grass. Their legs are not designed for fast running but enable the wolves to move easily through the grass while they are stalking their prey. When they sense danger, their mane bristles and they roar loudly so that other members of the pack know to beware.

▲ Maned wolves have large ears, which help them hear prey moving in long grass. They stalk their victim before pouncing at it when they are close enough.

Hunting their victims

Domesticated chickens are one of the most common victims of maned wolves, which they attack on farms. These wolves will also hunt down small grassland creatures, including rodents, snakes, and birds, and will attack humans if they come into their territory. Once they catch their victim, they hold it down with their front paws while they tear into the victim's flesh with their sharp teeth. A female maned wolf with new pups is known to be very aggressive to anyone who comes too close to her litter.

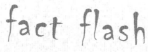

fact flash

The maned wolf is neither a wolf nor a fox, although its face is fox-like and its name sounds like it is a wolf.

Black-footed ferrets

VITAL STATISTICS

LENGTH
up to 12 inches
(31 cm)

WEIGHT
up to two pounds
(1 kg)

WHERE FOUND
central North
America

Black-footed ferrets may look cute and cuddly but they are dangerous to the prairie dogs that live in central United States. These ferrets, which are the rarest native mammal in the U.S., take over the tunnels of the prairie dogs. They attack the prairie dogs from these dark burrows and use their tunnels as dens for their own young. The female ferrets dig out the tunnels with their sharp claws to make them bigger, then look after their babies, called kits, there.

Strong support

Black-footed ferrets have a small head with strong muscles to support their neck, which enables them to tear apart large chunks of meat. Their sharp claws, strong jaws, and long, skinny body covered in short, brown hair are characteristic of the **mustelid** family, which they belong to. Because they spend much of their time in tunnels, they mostly hunt in the dark. Sometimes packs of prairie dogs will attack a ferret before it gets to them, leaving it with bad wounds.

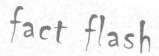

fact flash

By 2010, biologists hope to have 1,500 ferrets living in 10 groups in the wild, with 30 breeding adults among each group.

◄ Black-footed ferrets use the tunnels of the prairie dogs, which form an underground network, to travel across the plains.

fact flash

Native American tribes had different beliefs about the black-footed ferret. The Navajo nation used ferret body parts and skins in medicine and as ceremonial decorations. The Cheyenne and Blackfoot tribes decorated their chief's headdresses with the furs.

Fighting the enemy

Once a black-footed ferret senses the prairie dog is close, it grabs it with its sharp claws and bites into its neck with its cutting teeth and strong jaw. Black-footed ferrets nearly died out a few years ago because many prairie dogs, which they live off of, were killed by farmers. Breeding projects have been set up to help the black-footed ferret kits survive to an age when they can breed themselves.

▲ The black-footed ferret has a flexible backbone running right down its back, which makes it easier for the ferret to fit down narrow tunnels.

Tsetse flies

Tsetse flies are dangerous to animals and humans, not because of their bite but because of the deadly **parasites** they carry from victim to victim in their saliva. There are over twenty species of tsetse fly. They carry many different types of parasites, called trypanosomes. These are simple life forms and they live in the blood of other animals. One type causes sleeping sickness in humans, a disease that attacks the nervous system. An adult tsetse fly develops from a **pupa**, which has grown from a **larva**.

▲ A tsetse fly sucks up blood from its victim via its mouth. It lands on the skin then punctures the long tube part of its mouth, called a proboscis, into the skin's surface.

Deadly carrier

If a tsetse fly bites someone with blood that is infected with a trypanosome, this parasite travels into the fly's **salivary gland**. Then when the fly bites someone else, its infected **saliva** is passed on to that person. The trypanosome parasite is injected into their bloodstream, which causes the sleeping sickness to spread. Once people are infected, they develop a headache and a rash, then they become delirious before falling into a coma and dying. If people can be treated early, they can be cured of the disease.

fact flash

Scientists have found that zebras are invisible to tsetse flies—the zebra's stripes confuse the flies.

DANGER REPORT

In 2001, over 300 scientists met in Burkina, western Africa, to launch a fundraising campaign which would help wipe out the tsetse fly. It was hoped that mass testing centers for sleeping sickness could be set up in the rural areas of Africa, supported by donations from international drug companies.

Silent killer

Sleeping sickness is one of the most deadly diseases in Africa. Over 3,800,000 square miles are infested with tsetse flies, which cause over 100,000 Africans to be infected with the disease every year. Many people in remote rural areas could have sleeping sickness without realising it because they cannot be tested.

▲ A tsetse fly grows from a pupa into a fly under the ground. It digs its way to the surface once it is fully grown.

fact flash

A tsetse fly drinks up to three times its body weight in blood when it attacks its victim.

Eastern brown snakes

Eastern brown snakes are dangerous to humans as well as animals because they inject their victims with a deadly **venom**. These snakes live around bushland in the eastern half of Australia but like to hunt in the open grasslands. They hunt during the day, except sometimes in summer when it gets too hot. Their brown and orange colorings help them blend into their surroundings, but when they rear up and take on their striking pose they look very threatening, and are hard to miss.

Deadly striker

Eastern brown snakes bite more people in Australia than all of the other snakes put together. But they usually attack humans only if they are annoyed. They will often bite their victims more than once before the victim realises that they have been bitten. The snake injects its venom into the victim through two short **fangs**. The venom is stored in venom sacs behind its eyes. When the snake gets angry, it spreads its neck so that it is very noticeable, just like the Indian cobra does.

fact flash

Male snakes often compete for the right to mate during the mating season by displaying their strength. They wind their bodies around each other, then try to force each other's head to the ground.

▶ Mice and other rodents often fall victim to the eastern brown snake. It holds its prey with its body so that the prey cannot escape.

fact flash

When an eastern brown snake eats larger prey, as well injecting it with venom, it coils its body around its victim and constricts it, like a boa or python does.

Fatal dose

Once these snakes bite their victims they hold on until the victim is paralyzed, then they swallow their prey whole. Although the amount of venom it injects is small, the level of poison in this small amount is very high. Stomach pains, dizziness, and vomiting will start within moments of being bitten and victims usually need to be given an **antivenin** to stop them from dying.

▲ An eastern brown snake will twist its body into an "S" shape and lift up to one-third of it off the ground as it prepares to strike.

Endangered animals
of the
grasslands

More than 5,000 animal species in the world today are endangered. They are in danger from their competitors and predators, and they are in danger from natural disasters, such as droughts, floods, and fires.

But the greatest threat to animals comes from the most dangerous animals of all—humans. As more and more people fill the Earth, there is less room for wildlife. Humans clear land to put up buildings. They farm land for crops or grazing, or they mine it to produce fuel. Precious wildlife habitats are destroyed.

Here are just some of the animals that are in danger of vanishing forever from the grasslands of this planet.

ENDANGERED ANIMAL	WHERE FOUND
African wild dog	Southern east Africa
Black-footed ferret	Central North America
Black rhinoceros	Central and eastern Africa
Cuvier's gazelle	Northern Africa
Grevy's zebra	Eastern Africa
Indian bison	India
Indian elephant	India
Komodo dragon	Indonesia
Northern hairy-nosed wombat	Northeastern Australia
Pygmy hippopotamus	West Africa

You can find out more about saving the world's wildlife by visiting the World Wildlife Fund (WWF) at http://www.panda.org.

Glossary

antivenin the medicine given to someone bitten by a venomous animal to stop the venom from hurting them

camouflage something in an animal's appearance that helps it to blend into the background

carnivores animals that eat meat

clan a group of animals, such as hyenas, who live together

dung the droppings of an animal

fangs long, sharp, hollow teeth that are used by snakes to inject venom

food chain the relationship between living things. It shows which animals eat which in order to survive

habitat an animal's natural living place

herbivores animals that eat only plants

hibernate to completely rest during Winter, often underground

lairs the dens or shelters of animals

larva the young of an insect before it starts to grow into an adult

mammals animals whose young feed on their mother's milk

migrate to move in a particular season from one habitat to another

mustelid the name of the family of small, short-haired, meat-eating creatures with long bodies, such as ferrets

nocturnal sleeping by day and being active at night

omnivores animals that eat both plants and meat

parasites animals that live and feed on another living animal

predators animals that hunt and kill other animals

prey animals that are caught and eaten by other animals

pride a group of lions living together

pupa the stage of growth of an insect after it is a larva and before it becomes an adult

raptors one of the main groups of birds of prey, with hooked bills, strong feet, sharp talons, and large eyes

rodents the group of gnawing or nibbling mammals, such as rats and mice

saliva the liquid produced in the mouth by the salivary glands

salivary gland a body part that produces liquid in the mouth. The liquid helps animals to swallow and digest food

scavengers animals that feed off dead animals

sensory organs parts of the body that belong to the senses, such as the eyes, ears, nose, and skin

stalks follows prey silently until ready to rush out and pounce

venom poison that is injected by some animals to attack their enemies

Index